YOUR STORY
DOES NOT DEFINE
YOU

A Healing Journey from Trauma Through Expression and Self-Affirmation

Niesha Davis, MSW, LCSW, CAMS-II, CCTP

CHRISTIAN LIVING
B O O K S

Largo, MD

D1572673

© 2022 Niesha Davis

Christian Living Books, Inc.
P. O. Box 7584
Largo, MD 20792
christianlivingbooks.com
We bring your dreams to fruition.

ISBN 9781562295677

Dedication

This book is dedicated to some special people in my life who have kept me going. You have had faith in me; you have always been there to support me and push me to be the risk-taker I am and move in crazy faith! I want to dedicate this book to my mother and father, Susie and Lee, who have raised me to become the woman I am today. You have instilled in me to be the best that I can be and to always strive for greatness. I love you! To my beautiful children, this is who I do it for. James, Jadin, and Jade, you are the reason I have always worked so hard and strived to be the best version of me for you. I was so blessed when God gave me each of you. You all bring a different flavor to my life, and I absolutely love your individuality and creativity. You are the best children anyone can ask for... hands down. Each day that I smile, it's because of you! I love you. To my brother and sister-in-law, Lamorris (aka Dewey) and Shama, thank you for always supporting, encouraging, and believing in me. Thank you for seeing my vision and believing in me when others wanted to see me fail. I love you! To my dearest niece and bonus daughter, Lacoya, you are the strongest young lady I know. Keep striving to accomplish your dreams. I love you! To Marcus, I appreciate you and all that you have been to me—my best friend, my confidant, my personal therapist, my motivator, and my rock. Thank you for always supporting me and pushing me to the next level. You saw in me what I did not see in myself. You expected me—and helped me—to rise to the occasion, and I thank you for that. You have had my back and had me from day one. I love you!

Endorsements

"This is such a timely and insightful work. People have experienced trauma at various levels and are affected differently. Niesha has the experience, dedication, and expertise to help the reader—and even the therapist—to understand self-sabotaging behavior. At times, we function in dysfunction as if it is normal; however, it is not. When faced with trauma and challenges, we are forced to take the necessary steps to become better by doing the work. Reading this book and applying the principles shared is indeed doing the work. Trauma victims are looking for a way out but don't understand how to pursue freedom. In this book, Niesha skillfully provides the tools to health and wholeness. I love what Niesha wrote in Chapter 3: "I no longer have to walk in procrastination and create problems for myself. I no longer have to engage in those behaviors that are not conducive to me living." She takes the reader on a journey to victory. Niesha shows us how to diminish triggers and pursue positivity. She profoundly teaches the reader that healing also starts with speaking life over yourself. This book is an essential resource that will be life-changing."

–Lady Vicki L. Kemp
Bestselling Author of *Better than Yesterday* and *Grace in Deep Water*

"Niesha Davis has seamlessly weaved support, guidance, and encouragement into the pages of this powerful book. As a life coach, I sometimes work with clients who are overwhelmed by the trauma they carry through life. This is a book I enthusiastically recommend to help empower the healing process forward for those who have experienced trauma. Niesha gives the reader the permission to heal that so many who are struggling in their process crave. Dive into this book and allow the words to guide you to your strongest and most empowered self yet."

–Miriam Isinini Popp, CWC
Owner of Vibrant Lifestyle Coaching

"I am honored to write this endorsement for Niesha, whom I have known since 2008. Our relationship grew from being colleagues as Social Service Workers to Licensed Clinical Social Workers providing psychotherapy. Niesha is not only a gifted writer, but she is also passionate about helping others heal from their trauma. This book will help you acknowledge the negative experiences that happened to you and empower you to break free from the fear that keeps you perpetually cycling in trauma."

–**Pamela Shakir, MSW, LCSW**
Author of *Creative Strategies: A Self-Guided Journal to Help You Kick Depression*

"This book is an empowering and compassionate read for anyone who has experienced trauma and is on their path toward healing. Niesha's words flow beautifully with such intention and courage as she shares tools and strategies as one walks their journey from trauma to healing. As Niesha writes, readers are not only able to be transparent with their story but also acknowledge that they are not alone in this journey we call life. This insightful tool provides space to release attachments to things, events, memories, and people that no longer serve them. By sharing her knowledge and expert insight, her text provides guidance and encouragement that is practical and relatable and will serve as a valuable asset to anyone who has experienced trauma as they navigate their own path toward healing and reclaiming hope, joy, and self-love."

–**Anastasia Locklin,** LMFT Founder of Unlock Your Joy Therapy

"As a licensed mental health therapist and Christian Empowerment Strategist, I find trauma to be a major issue in the lives of many. The complex, multifaceted nature of trauma hinders one's ability to move past their painful past and keeps them stuck in cyclic bouts of depression and anxiety. Niesha provides a blueprint to tackle trauma and gives us tools to move toward a healthy and healed life."

–**Dr. Antionette D. Brookins, PhD, LMFT**
Author of *The Anatomy of Anger: A Girl's Guide to Living Her Best Life in Christ*

Contents

Preface

This book is for all the strong individuals who made a conscientious effort to continue to live! Those who lived past the hurt and the pain of their life experiences. Those who fought through the tears, confusion, low self-esteem, low self-worth, guilt, regret, bad choices, rejection, abandonment, and uncontrollable circumstances that caused you to question your life and who you are. This book is dedicated to you because you chose to live and be a victor, not a victim. Know that I see you. I am proud of you, and I am rooting for you to continue to thrive! Pat yourself on the back and tell yourself, "My story does not define me."

This book is also for you, yes, you who are reading this book today! I see you too. I am rooting for you because you *can* do this! You got this! You are a victor, not a victim! You are strong. Repeat after me and say it again, "I am strong. I am a victor, not a victim. My story does not define me."

While reading this book, you will be challenged to start your healing journey through expression and self-affirmation. This book was strategically written for you to do the work it takes to start your healing journey. As you read this interactive book, you will be speaking to yourself. Allow yourself to be interwoven in the words and pages of this book. Challenge yourself to stand against fear and face dark places. Speak life to yourself. These steps will allow you to heal and move from a place of surviving to thriving!

Introduction

Life and life's challenges are inevitable—you cannot escape them. As long as you have breath in your body and are living, breathing, and moving, you will experience this thing called life. The extent and magnitude of your experiences are individualized and sometimes happen beyond your control. That means you did not choose to go through what you did. You did not choose to be violated, mistreated, misunderstood, taken advantage of, abused, rejected, abandoned, left for dead, hurt, or left to endure the pain that you did.

Your story may not be someone else's story. Your hurt and pain may not feel the same as theirs. However, the essence of the experience is undeniably yours and undeniably theirs. True healing can only happen when you identify the trauma that caused you hurt and pain. You must be willing to address it, process it, and begin to heal from it.

Trauma is defined as a deeply distressing, disturbing experience that causes an emotional response. It changes how you view yourself and others. It shapes your reality and shifts your core beliefs. Whether considered acute, chronic, or complex, its effects are crippling, debilitating, and silencing. Trauma silences you to the point at which you can block it out of your mind and pretend it never happened to you. Until the triggering effects haunt you and bring you back... back to relive the experience or experiences all over again. It forces you to open the wound you bandaged and hoped would heal on its own and go away. Not realizing that the scars left in your mind and on your body would only continue to hurt you and haunt you until you do the work to heal. That is until you endure the vigorous pain it takes to relive the traumatic experience from a different place and face the realities you tell yourself aren't true.

By this point, you may have already started to get triggered and may be experiencing feelings of anxiety. Don't worry—that's okay. Take some deep breaths (inhale/exhale 5-7-8). Regroup. Cry if you must because this is all part of the healing journey… and it's okay. Let the tears flow. The healing journey sometimes hurts more than the original experience. However, remember… You. Got. This. It's time for you to do the work! It's time for you to stop being imprisoned by what happened to you, what someone did to you, or what you may have even seen. It's time to break the chains and be free. It's time to live a life of liberty. Your story does not define you… you are a victor and not a victim! So, let's get to work!

"I see you, and I am rooting for you.
When it gets tough, remember… **YOU. GOT. THIS!***"*

CHAPTER 1

TODAY I DID A THING

So, today I did a thing… I made a decision. I finally decided to choose me over everyone and anything else. Yes, I did it! I chose to take my power back and no longer let my experiences have control over my mind, emotions, body, mental wellness, and choices.

I found the strength that I need to take this first step in defeating the torment that has gripped me with fear for so long. I've finally found the strength that I need to learn to love myself over what has victimized me. It may be just an ounce of strength, and I am barely moving. However, I've arrived at the beginning of my healing journey… and here I am, willing and ready to work towards being sound, whole, and restored.

Now that this step of courage has brought me here, there's so much I want to say and do for me, because I... yes, I... deserve to love and appreciate me! I deserve to rediscover those things that I've lost and live again. I have chosen to completely love me, let go of the past, and move forward. I have chosen not to be afraid and hurt again. I have chosen to heal me.

So, here I am, willing and ready to take the first step!

PAST

I am so proud of myself because I have chosen to look at things from a different perspective. I have chosen to shine through the darkness that I allowed to hover over me in a cloud hiding my sunshine and stagnating me from seeing my worth and value.

I will no longer wait until the storm passes. Instead, I choose to keep moving through the storm as it will pass. I am no longer going to live in my past. I have chosen to move forward. I know it may take some time, and some days will be better than others. Some days I may feel more energized to push, and others I may not. Nevertheless, I will not stop. I will continue to be invested in myself and my healing. It all starts today.

I can't wait to see where this journey will take me! Yes, I may get scared along the way, and yes, I may cry and remember hurtful things from the past or remember bad decisions that led me to a place of defeat. However, I will not be defeated any longer. Today, I am choosing to set myself free and live! So, here I am, willing and ready to take the first step!

Congratulations, you have consciously decided to face the dark cloud of denial, shame, and fear. You have chosen to admit what really happened to you or what you experienced that has been holding you back. Allow yourself to be honest and present with your feelings and emotions today.

Tell yourself what your trauma did to you. Why? I'm glad you asked! Trauma lives in your body. When you don't heal from it, you can easily be triggered all the time by people, places, and things. Those are chains that are holding you hostage. It's time to free yourself and break the chains. It's time for you to do the work.

CHAPTER CHALLENGE

What happened to you? What has imprisoned you? What has been holding you hostage? What has been keeping you from loving yourself? What has kept you from living a life of freedom and happiness? What are you blaming yourself for that you are willing to let go of today?

Write It Out

....

....

....

....

....

....

....

....

....

....

....

....

....

....

....

....

....

....

SELF-AFFIRMATION

Write out your own affirmation after reading this chapter. Make a commitment to challenge yourself to say it today and when you need to be reminded and reaffirmed.

....

....

....

....

....

....

....

CHAPTER 2

ONE TEAR AT A TIME

I can't begin to count the tears that I have cried. So many that I found myself drowning in! Sitting all alone when no one could see me, trying to find my way through the entanglement of thoughts in my mind, only to be blinded consistently by the unclear vision that I have been consumed with by my tears. Trying to make sense of it all and gain answers to the questions that have been unerasable in my mind. So many unanswered and unresolved feelings that were ignored or discredited or that just did not make sense to me.

Why did this happen to me? Why was I created to be this way? I didn't ask for this life and this family. Why couldn't things have been different? Why did they have to be taken away from me so soon? Why couldn't people just understand me? Why didn't they believe me? I thought they loved me. I just wanted to be loved and appreciated. Why did they hurt me? Why does life have to be so hard? Why did they reject me? Bad things always happen to me. Why me? Why was I left for dead?

Oh, the whys… yes, you can go on and on with the questions… the whys… trying to figure out the unsolved mysteries in your mind. Questioning God, "Why did You let those things happen to me?" The pain, the hurt… it's so hard and was so hard. It wasn't and it isn't fair! Yes, you can continue to allow yourself to be a victim and allow your tears to consume you. Or you can continue to cry one tear at a time, learn to admit that you are broken, and cry your way to healing! No, crying isn't a bad thing… it's a release. It's a coping mechanism that you can choose to use for your betterment. Instead of drowning in your tears, swim to safety.

You may even be crying now, and that's okay. Cry. Cry. Cry. Let it out! There is healing in your tears! Crying allows you to become vulnerable and helps connect you with your deepest feelings and emotions. It helps you to move from a place of denial to acceptance of those feelings. That is a segue of release you need to move forward.

It allows you to let go of the baggage of pain

and suffering you have endured and gives you the strength you need to release fear and be strong!

When you cry, tears help release toxins from your body. So, envision your tears releasing those toxins from your traumatic experience that caused you the hurt and the pain. Cleanse yourself from what happened to you. Don't get stuck in the guilt and the shame. Instead, be vulnerable and let the tears flow! Crying is not just beneficial for an improved mood. It decreases stress and anxiety and is also beneficial to your physical health as the limbic system will allow your brain and heart to feel good again! It helps with decreasing blood pressure. Tears talk when you can't speak or find the words to say. Crying is a form of communication that helps process your emotions. Crying brings instant relief and restoration. Crying gets you back to your baseline of functioning.

Instead of drowning in your tears, swim to safety.

Don't be ashamed. We are human with human feelings and emotions. Crying is a part of our genetic makeup. So, let those tears flow, one tear at a time. Let them flow and find yourself releasing.

CHAPTER CHALLENGE

What do you find yourself crying about, and why? What can you envision and allow to be released from your traumatic experience when you cry?

Write It Out

....

....

....

....

....

....

....

....

....

....

....

....

....

....

....

....

....

....

....

....

Affirmation
"Tears are not a sign of weakness, but
of courage. Hiding your emotions
is self-destructive and will
never allow you to heal."
—Author Unknown

SELF-AFFIRMATION

Write out your own affirmation after reading this chapter. Make a commitment to challenge yourself to say it today and when you need to be reminded and reaffirmed.

....

....

....

....

....

....

CHAPTER 3

NO MORE SELF-SABOTAGING... CONNECT THE DOTS

Today is the day that I stop allowing myself to be the cause of my own destruction. No longer will I question myself and have a negative perception of me. I no longer have to be afraid of those thoughts that torment me day in and day out, but I will stand up to them and take my power back! I no longer have to pretend those things didn't happen to me, but I will stand up to the truth and reality. I no longer have to feel less than and worthless, but I see myself as worthy.

I am worthy of life, love, peace, relationships, happiness, and so much more. I don't have to settle. I don't have to continue to have a pity party for myself. I don't have to be afraid to fail or feel like a failure. Everyone makes mistakes and experiences challenges.

I no longer have to walk in procrastination and create problems for myself. I no longer have to engage in those behaviors that are not conducive to me living. I don't have to cut to numb the pain. I don't have to self-medicate to make it go away. I don't have to overeat or eat to feel comforted. I don't have to be a perfectionist to appease others and make them feel good. I no longer have to be impulsive and do things that I regret later.

I don't have to be abused or abuse my body and my mind as they have value. I no longer have to shut my mouth in fear as there is power in my words. I no longer have to suppress my feelings because they are important and deserve attention. I no longer have to wish to die or disappear or attempt to end my life. My life is worth living!

I will learn to know me, love me, and know my triggers.

I will no longer sabotage myself! I will learn to know me, love me, and know my triggers. I am choosing to grow! I will set goals for myself. I am choosing to be proactive and fight for my life!

Yaaaaaasssss! That's right, say that! I hear you! Speak life to yourself! No longer do you have to stand in your own way. This is the day that you can stop contributing to your own self-destruction through self-sabotage.

You have the power to connect the dots. What do I mean by that? Learn your triggers. Learn what you are doing, thinking, and saying to yourself that does not promote your life's healing and productivity. Some thoughts and actions happen automatically without you being completely aware of them. However, take a daily self-inventory and really get to know you.

Know when you are feeling over-whelmed, stressed, and not just feeling your best. Know when traumatic experiences are sending signals to your body because something reminded you of what happened (remember, trauma lives in your body). Know your surroundings and the environments that make you feel uneasy (people, places, things, items,

A L E R T

and dates). Why? So that you can be proactive. This is connecting the dots! This is identifying and knowing what your triggers are— and knowing your body's stress response.

Triggers are your warning sign. They are the flashing red lights that send signals to let your body know that something doesn't feel right, or you aren't in a good place. You may sweat or have a rapid heart rate. Your digestive system may shift. The more you are aware and know about yourself and know your body's stress response, the more you will learn how to help yourself transition. And, the sooner your healing will take place. The fear and pain that gripped you will release their hold, and the wounds can continue to heal.

I know it sounds scary and seems like a lot of work. You can take one day at a time. Take your time. There is no rush as you are the only one who truly understands your hurt and pain. However, remember that healing from trauma is work. The healing process is sometimes more painful than the traumatic experience itself. Don't be afraid to think about whatever it is. You can conquer and defeat it because you are strong even when you feel weak. Say it: "I am strong!" Yes, you absolutely are. Find the courage that you need to be transparent. Talk about those painful experiences and emotions and do the work. You are stronger than you think you are… YOU. GOT. THIS!

CHAPTER CHALLENGE

How are you self-sabotaging yourself? What behaviors are you engaging in that are contributing to your self-destruction? What negative thoughts do you keep telling yourself that you will release? What have you blocked out of your mind that you will be honest about?

Write It Out

....

....

....

....

....

....

....

....

....

....

....

....

....

....

....

....

SELF-AFFIRMATION

Write out your own affirmation after reading this chapter. Make a commitment to challenge yourself to say it today and when you need to be reminded and reaffirmed.

....

....

....

....

....

....

CHAPTER 4

FORGIVENESS AND RECONCILIATION

W hy do I have to be the one to say sorry? Why do I have to be the one to forgive when they did this to me? I did not ask for this... I did not choose this... This is not my fault... I hate myself... I know I messed up... I made a bad decision... If they had never done that, I wouldn't be dealing with this now... If things had been different, then I would be different... They haven't even said "I'm sorry" or acknowledged they're wrong... I really don't understand why he/she could do that to me and say that to me... My mother/father hurt me. How could they?!? I do forgive them, but I can't forget it. It still hurts...

The list of what-ifs can go on and on. You can go on forever about how things could have been different. You can point the finger and blame others. You can blame yourself for what may have gone wrong or for what may have happened to you. However, STOP IT! STOP IT NOW! Because it will not get you anywhere or resolve anything.

It's time to move on and let it go.

It's time to move on and let it go. Yes, I know this is easier said than done, but you have to forgive them and forgive yourself in order to heal. I know it doesn't make sense. No, you don't have to be their friend or talk to them. However, you do have to forgive for reconciliation to happen within you. And, you do have to continue to love.

Forgiveness is not just for the person who violated you. Forgiveness is for YOU! I know it hurts and things were bad and are bad... They may have left you for dead... You may really regret what you did... You may feel ashamed and guilty and disappointed about what you did... You may not completely understand why someone would say or do that to you... Maybe it was your mom, dad, another family member, friend, or even a stranger... LET IT GO! Free yourself and free your mind! For you!

Let go of blaming yourself and being mad at yourself. We are not perfect. We are human, and we ALL make mistakes and miss the mark. Stupid choices, failures, and unwise decisions are the source of our growth. How will we know to make it right if we never did anything wrong? No perfect people allowed.

The reality is that it may even be easier to forgive the person who hurt you as you have found a way to make the situation *your* fault. You may be living with the blame, guilt, and shame as you have completely owned it. You feel like you blew it and ruined everything! Forgiving yourself can be more challenging.

When you don't forgive, you deal with mental anguish such as anger, which becomes bitter and numb. Eventually, it will affect your physical health, and illness can strike your body. Unforgiveness stagnates you and holds you back. It places a roadblock in your way. No matter how hard you try to go around it, it will still be there.

Unforgiveness stagnates you and holds you back.

Take a moment to pause and think about what you are holding on to. Don't be afraid to admit that you blew it. Don't be afraid to admit what happened to you, even if it wasn't your fault. Let the tight fist of fear go and relinquish that unforgiveness. You will feel much better! As you let it go and forgive others and yourself, you will realize that it is a lot easier than you imagined. It may take some time but do it! Don't live with regret.

Reconciliation in the Greek language means to "change completely". As you begin to forgive others and forgive yourself, you will see change happening right before your eyes. You will begin to feel much lighter and brighter. You will find an appreciation for yourself. Know that your mistakes and trauma are not the definitions of who you are or what society says you should be. However, letting go and moving forward will be the fuel to push you forward. Life is too short. Don't let your bad decisions or what happened to you be your excuse to lay down and die. Let it be the reason that you rise above it all. Be resilient and live with purpose and passion. Thrive! FORGIVE... It will save your life.

CHAPTER CHALLENGE

What are you holding onto that you need to let go of? Who do you need to forgive? What do you need to forgive yourself for?

Write It Out

....

....

....

....

....

....

....

....

....

....

....

....

....

....

....

....

....

....

Affirmation

"Forgiveness of the self is just
as important as forgiving others."
—Author Unknown

SELF-AFFIRMATION

Write out your own affirmation after reading this chapter. Make a commitment to challenge yourself to say it today and when you need to be reminded and reaffirmed.

....

....

....

....

....

....

....

....

....

....

CHAPTER 5

DON'T BE SILENT

Silence is how I have managed to walk through life. Silence is how I have managed to deal with my pain. Silence has muted my voice and stopped me from expressing my genuine emotions when I wanted to speak up. Being silent is what I was told to do to protect my abuser from getting in trouble or being exposed. Being silent is how I mask my true hurt and pain and shut the world out of my reality.

Silence has been the leading factor in my mental torment and daily struggle to stay alive. Silence has kept me from being embarrassed and feeling ashamed of others knowing my truth. Silence has been my coping mechanism and has been my comforter. Silence has been my escape! Silence has blocked my expression. Silence has suppressed all the things within me. Silence has been and sometimes continues to be my go-to.

Silence prohibits one from speaking and suppresses and prevents one from expressing their truth. Silence has been the muzzle over one's mouth to limit transparency and honesty with self. Silence is a quiet killer that consumes a person's life and very existence. Silence is a trick of the enemy to take you out.

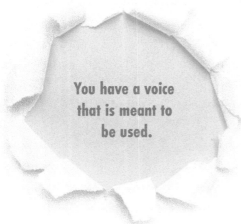

You have a voice that is meant to be used.

Stop being silent and open your mouth! You no longer have to suffer in silence. You no longer have to be muted. You no longer have to hide behind your silence. You have a voice that is meant to be used. So, open your mouth and speak up and free yourself. Free yourself from all the torment and fear that has gripped you. Free yourself from the agony of failure to allow yourself to speak.

Silence is the absence of sound. And, without sound, one can't hear. Your words have power. When you speak, the very core of the atmosphere shifts like an earthquake. You have the power to change your reality through what you speak. Your words can break curses because your perception and attitude will change. When you speak over negativity and replace it with positive words, you tear down the darkness and shed light on your situation. You are tearing down walls that you have built up to go into hiding, to shelter yourself from any hurt and pain. You are hiding from the very essence of the source of your pain, trying to remain strong and smile through the silent agony. You cry behind closed doors and continue to fight battles that nobody knows you fight.

The more you speak positivity over your life, the more it will take root in your heart. Positivity will create a new belief system that will restore or change your core beliefs. The more you share your story, the more you unlock the shackles that have imprisoned you. You will begin to think and feel better about yourself. You will begin living in a whole new world for yourself with a sense of liberality that has blossomed from the seeds you planted. You will free yourself from the silence that has been so loud.

When you hold things in, you become entangled in a battle within yourself and your mind. Guess what? Your mind gets the best of you. The negative thoughts will ruminate. The lies that have formed will appear to be true. This is the formula for an ultimate shut down and break down. I challenge you to stop hiding your vulnerabilities and allow yourself to be the human you are.

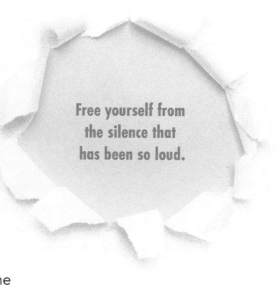

Free yourself from the silence that has been so loud.

We are creatures who long for affection and love and desire a sense of belonging. Conquer your fears of rejection, being judged, feeling misunderstood, and isolation. The memories of what happened to you may never go away, but don't let them be the definition of your life. Learn to connect with others around you again. Cling to those who love you, bring you joy and happiness, and make you feel good. Yes, the pain hurts. However, the water will recede, and the storm will subside. The love, joy, and happiness will drown the hurt and pain caused by your traumatic experience—whether great or small.

Share your story because someone needs to hear it. You need to be validated, and so do they. You made it through to help someone else and being silent will rob you of your testimony. We heal when we reveal. Someone understands you, and someone wants to support you. You don't have to suffer in silence. So, break the silence!

CHAPTER CHALLENGE

What has kept you silent? What are you willing to reveal to heal?
How can you break your silence?

Write It Out

....

....

....

....

....

....

....

....

....

....

....

....

....

....

....

....

....

....

....

....

Affirmation
"Don't suffer in silence."
—Author Unknown

SELF-AFFIRMATION

Write out your own affirmation after reading this chapter. Make a commitment to challenge yourself to say it today and when you need to be reminded and reaffirmed.

....

....

....

....

....

....

....

....

....

....

CHAPTER 6

CREATE BOUNDARIES

"Daring to set boundaries is about having the courage to love ourselves, even when we risk disappointing others." –Brené Brown

Who said that I have to stop communicating with people who hurt me during the healing process? Who said that I have to be mean towards them and stop loving them? Who said healing means I have to accept less than and that I can't shine like the diamond I am? Who said that I have to take on a different identity after trauma and change my core beliefs? Who said that I have to change who I am? Who said I am not important or valuable? I don't have to change my core beliefs. I am still valuable!

It's called setting boundaries. What are boundaries? I'm glad you asked. Boundaries are set in place to allow you to regain a sense of who you are and what you are. You need boundaries to help you to be safe. Boundaries are your security blanket after enduring whatever your traumatic experience has been. Boundaries help with restoring your self-worth and self-esteem. Boundaries are essential to your healing journey and recovery, and they demand respect.

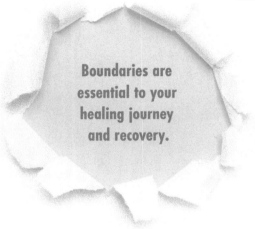

Boundaries are essential to your healing journey and recovery.

After being violated, we feel less than or like damaged goods. Boundaries are part of you restoring trust for others and, most importantly, yourself. Creating healthy boundaries will help restore and renew you after you feel like there is no coming back. You can gain your good name back. You are worthy of being loved. You deserve healthy relationships and friendships. You are more than your circumstance and what you have done. You are more than what was done or said to you and about you. You can and will set healthy boundaries. You will be consistent with setting them.

Don't let your trauma keep you silent and cause you to hide out of fear. You have been at a place before where your boundaries were violated. That caused you to be angry and frustrated. That made you feel like you were not in control. It made you feel uncomfortable. Nevertheless, rise above it. Allow yourself to gain control back over your life and over yourself. Enforce those boundaries.

"I respect my boundaries, and I insist that
others respect them too." –Louise Hay

You may be wondering, "Well, how do I do that?" You do it by making some changes. First, identify that you deserve to be respected, loved, and feel safe. Boundaries are personal as they are set based on your feelings and emotions. Boundaries belong to you and no one else. You are the owner of your boundaries, and you create the rules!

Don't be afraid to defend yourself. Don't be afraid to say no. Don't be afraid to pursue your desires and what you feel makes you happy. Don't be afraid to limit your conversations with someone because they don't make you feel good when talking to them or they trigger you. Don't be afraid to separate yourself from people who don't serve you anymore, or who are not bringing positivity, joy, and support to your life. No, it doesn't mean that you have to dislike them or hate them as boundaries are not unkind, and they are not electric fences.

It just means that you can pick and choose how you allow yourself to show up in someone's life and how you will allow them to show up in yours. Don't be afraid to let go!

Boundaries can be easy to set. However, it may be difficult to remain consistent. Remember… You. Got. This! You can do it. Never forget that boundaries are for you first—to keep *you* SAFE. Boundaries help you to regain your sense of self-worth, love, and direction. Boundaries will help you with moving from a place of surviving to thriving. Boundaries help you to recognize that you are worthy, and you value your needs and feelings. Boundaries help you release feelings as if the responsibility of how others feel or behave is yours.

Focus on what you can control and be intentional about setting your boundaries. Write them out if that helps you process what healthy boundaries look like for you. Know your values and what is important to you. Boundaries are to be created by you and set for you, your family, friendships, work relationships, intimate relationships, and strangers. Remember… you need boundaries on this healing journey. You. Got. This!

CHAPTER CHALLENGE

What boundaries do you need to set? How will you set those boundaries? How will you remain consistent?

Write It Out

....

....

....

....

....

....

....

....

....

....

....

....

....

....

....

....

....

....

....

Affirmation
"The only people who get upset
when you set boundaries are
the ones who benefited
from you having none."
—Author Unknown

SELF-AFFIRMATION

Write out your own affirmation after reading this chapter. Make a commitment to challenge yourself to say it today and when you need to be reminded and reaffirmed.

....

....

....

....

....

....

SHOW UP FOR YOURSELF... COPING AND HEALING

"80% of success is just showing up." –Woody Allen

The fact that you purchased this book and made it to Chapter 7 is evidence that you are serious about your healing journey from your trauma. Whatever your trauma is—whether it appears small or great in the eyes of others—it is significant to you. You made it this far, so smile. Pat yourself on the back and do a little dance because you are showing up for you! I am proud of you... I am smiling with you. Don't stop here—keep showing up for you every day.

Whether your healing journey takes six months or six years, don't stop. Only you know the significance of your hurt and pain. Only you know the thoughts you sit with daily—the thoughts that haunt and torment you. So, take your time and continue to heal one day at a time. No one can date stamp your healing. Just know that you will feel good again no matter how long it takes. You can feel happy with yourself and about yourself if you keep moving forward. Don't allow yourself to become afraid. Don't put the bandage that was covering your wound back on because it hurts. Look at your wound as a reminder that you showed up for yourself and are an overcomer. Continue to heal. Let that be your reminder to keep going.

We have covered several things in the previous chapters that may have triggered you. We've got you thinking, have you being honest with yourself, and pushing and challenging you to keep fighting... to keep rising up for you.

You have the power to make this healing journey a success.

The first step to healing is identifying the trauma. You've got to understand and know that you need to heal. You also must want to heal from it, be willing to get help, and accept the support. You have accomplished that first step and have made other steps thus far. You are in the driver's seat. You have the power to make this healing journey a success. So, make it happen because you have shown up.

So, exactly how do you truly show up for yourself and how do you cope to heal? You make steps every day, that is how. You make a conscious choice every day that you breathe the breath of life and make the best choices for you. Know who you are. Trust the choices you make and have compassion and grace for yourself. When no one is there cheering you on—or giving you the support you need—show up and cheer yourself on! Be your number one fan and cheerleader. Wake up every day with purpose and on purpose. Shower, get dressed, comb your hair, and feel good about being alive and in your skin. Do this no matter what you are going through. Show up with understanding and unconditional love for yourself. Be unbothered. Live unapologetically. Take care of your physical and mental health… YOU MATTER!

Know the coping mechanisms that can help keep you grounded and focused. In case you are struggling with what to do, here are a few tips:

- ❤ Affirm yourself daily—speak life to yourself (aloud)
- ❤ Push beyond the pressure
- ❤ Seek professional help
- ❤ Engage in mindfulness, activities, or meditation
- ❤ Do physical movement
- ❤ Practice self-care
- ❤ Connect yourself with positive people who bring positive energy
- ❤ Continue to process your feelings

- ❤ Be honest and transparent with yourself
- ❤ Remember, this is not a race. Take your time
- ❤ Read a book
- ❤ Relax (whatever that looks like for you)
- ❤ Find a new hobby
- ❤ Practice gratitude daily
- ❤ Get a proper amount of sleep and rest
- ❤ Do more things that you enjoy

These are just a few ways to show up for yourself. However, I encourage you to think of other ways to meet your individual situation and needs. Whatever you decide to do, just Show Up for You Because You Matter!

CHAPTER CHALLENGE

How will you show up for yourself every day? What things will you do to help you cope? How will you continuously show up for yourself as you heal?

Write It Out

....

....

....

....

....

....

....

....

....

....

....

....

....

....

....

....

....

....

....

....

Affirmation

"Show up in every single moment like you're meant to be there."

—Marie Forleo

SELF-AFFIRMATION

Write out your own affirmation after reading this chapter. Make a commitment to challenge yourself to say it today and when you need to be reminded and reaffirmed.

....

....

....

....

....

....

....

CHAPTER 8

RELAX

Release, Exhale, Letting All things Xscape! Repeat... Release, Exhale, Letting All things Xscape!

RELAX in more ways than one. Allow yourself to release all the tension you have been holding on to. Decrease those feelings of anxiety and fear that have gripped you so tightly. Chill out, decompress, and allow yourself to feel the calm.

I know you have been stuck in heightened awareness. Your muscles have been tight and rigid. Your brain has been programmed into survival mode. You have been on autopilot because you feel as if you have lost control. One of the goals on this healing journey from trauma is gaining your sense of control back. Relaxing will do just that. Relaxing will help train you to have great influence over your physical and emotional being.

Grant yourself permission to release and let go.

Traumatic experiences, whether great or small, take from your physical, emotional, and mental energy. Learn to be compassionate and gracious with yourself. Grant yourself permission to release and let go. It will help you to take control and relax. It will rejuvenate you and increase your energy. Remember, trauma lives in our bodies and affects our nervous system. The past does not control your present, and there is nothing wrong with you.

RELEASE

Set yourself free. Allow yourself to escape the confinement of the thoughts holding you captive. You have the keys to your own mental prison. So, unlock the door and set yourself free. Your parole date has arrived.

EXHALE

Breathe out! You have inhaled all the things that have happened to you. And, you have been holding your breath without breathing out. Inhaling and exhaling—the process of gas exchange—is an essential part of life. So, whatever negativity, fear, rejection, abuse, or bad choices have happened to you, inhale them and exhale freedom from it all. We cannot physically live without breathing. Breathing requires inhaling and exhaling. Take one breath at a time. This helps relax the body. You cannot heal from your trauma until you exhale!

LETTING ALL THINGS

Let it go... Let it all go! Letting go is not forgetting. It's allowing yourself not to be consumed with the things that have happened to you or what you have done. Quit dwelling on whatever it was and is and let it go. We have all experienced some type of hurt and pain. Your pain may definitely have been more traumatic and have affected you more severely than someone else's. Let me validate your feelings. Yes, it hurt. Yes, it was wrong. Yes, you made a mistake. Yes, you didn't ask for it. It is unfair, and it is not right. You have sat with that because you have every right to feel the way you have and do. You have been sad and angry and may still be. However, it's time to let it all go. Sitting with your pain and your past has become a familiar place. You may have learned to cope there even if it's been negative and painful. Letting go forces you to move to a space of the unknown, which can be scary. However, I challenge you to allow yourself to be vulnerable, embrace it, and start moving towards what's ahead. Your future is much brighter. Take responsibility for all mistakes made and confront any unresolved painful memories. There is no space for what was, in your what is and will be! Let go of it ALL!

XSCAPE

Stop avoiding the inevitable and move from confinement. If you want to heal from trauma, you have to do the work. You have purpose. The sooner you know and accept that, the sooner you will realize that you have work to do and will get to work. Xscape all negativity and negative thoughts. Someone needs to hear your story. They will never hear it if you don't allow yourself the liberty to share it.

> "If we can just let go and trust that things
> will work out the way they're supposed to,
> without trying to control the outcome,
> then we can begin to enjoy the moment
> more fully. The joy of the freedom it
> brings becomes more pleasurable than
> the experience itself." –Goldie Hawn

CHAPTER CHALLENGE

What have you been struggling to let go of? How will you allow yourself to RELAX?

Write It Out

....

....

....

....

....

....

....

....

....

....

....

....

....

....

....

....

....

....

....

Affirmation
"I Exhale. I Release. I Let Go."
—Author Unknown

SELF-AFFIRMATION

Write out your own affirmation after reading this chapter. Make a commitment to challenge yourself to say it today and when you need to be reminded and reaffirmed.

CHAPTER 9

YOU HAVE SURVIVED TO THRIVE

I made it. I survived. I lived through the hurt, the pain, the lone-liness. I made it past being misunderstood, feeling less than, feeling unworthy, feeling rejected and unloved. I survived. I lived to see another day. It was hard, and some days I was floating on my broken pieces. Some days I didn't know how I would make it through. I thought I was going to drown in my agony and tears. Yet, I'm here. When I attempted to end my life or wanted to end my life, I thought I would be successful. But I'm here to keep liv-ing and tell my story. Yes, I survived, even though I don't always understand why I had to go through what I did. I am still here.

> **I will position my mindset to growth and development.**

Some days, it is still hard and I'm still trying to beat the odds stacked against me. I am living to be able to tell the story of how I overcame these unbelievable circumstances. I'm living to testify about how my life changed forever because I survived. I'm not dead. I am alive and breathing and am still existing. I am a survivor! There has to be a purpose for my existence. I will wrap my mind around the fact that there is purpose for my life. Even when I cannot make sense of it all, there must be a reason why I am still here.

So, today I am choosing not to work towards surviving each day. Instead, I will work towards thriving. I will grow and I will flourish. I will be prosperous in every way possible. I will position my mindset to growth and development. I will make steps—then strides—forward. I will hold my head up high and not be ashamed of what happened to me. I will live to not just merely exist, but moreover to thrive!

Yes, you made it this far! Resilient, that's you! You've done and are doing what others have not done. What you did or what happened to you did not overtake you. You are alive to continue to live. Don't just live and exist but find your ticket and get on the plane to thrive.

You are unique and valuable and deserve to think positively about yourself. You deserve to live a life that brings you joy and happiness. You deserve to focus on yourself and the things that make you feel good. You can move from the past and focus on your future and what you like and admire about yourself.

Listen to your inner voice. Pay attention to the signals that are pushing you to greatness. Drown out the negative voices. Challenge all the negative thoughts. See your inner strength and choose your thoughts carefully. You are stronger than what you think you are, and the best is yet to come. Forgive yourself and others and all your past mistakes. Know that your tests and trials come to make you strong. Without a test, there is no testimony. Everything you have been through has proven that you have been able to stand. Even though the ground got shaky and you fell, you got back up and kept going. You survived, and you will thrive.

Focus on thriving by being aware of how your trauma affects and has affected you. Stay in the moment, be present, and stay focused. Discipline yourself. Know that you will fall and make mistakes along the way. You may even backslide. However, don't stay there— keep going. Dust yourself off and keep moving forward.

"Quitters never win, and winners never quit." Be 100% accountable and responsible for you. There is no room for others to dismiss you when you are completely in charge of your life. You thrive when you survive. You thrive when you arrive! You have arrived, and now that you are doing the work, you survived to thrive. Now thrive!

"Note: don't just exist, live."
–Author Unknown

"And once the storm is over, you won't
remember how you made it through,
how you managed to survive. You won't even
be sure whether the storm is really over.
But one thing is certain. When you come out of
the storm, you won't be the same person who
walked in. That's what this storm is all about."
–From *Kafka on the Shore* by Haruki Murakami

CHAPTER CHALLENGE

What have you survived? How can you move from a place of surviving to one of thriving?

Write It Out

....

....

....

....

....

....

....

....

....

....

....

....

....

....

....

....

....

....

....

Affirmation
"My mission in life is not merely
to survive, but to thrive; and to do
so with some passion, some
compassion, some humor,
and some style."
—Maya Angelou

SELF-AFFIRMATION

Write out your own affirmation after reading this chapter. Make a commitment to challenge yourself to say it today and when you need to be reminded and reaffirmed.

....

....

....

....

....

....

CHAPTER 10

MY STORY DOES NOT DEFINE ME

"Healing doesn't have to look magical or pretty. Real healing is hard, exhausting, and draining. Let yourself go through it. Don't try to paint it as anything other than what it is. Be there for yourself with no judgment." –Author Unknown

What you have experienced or have been through does not define who you are. It doesn't define your sense of self or self-worth. You don't have to be the hero of your own story because you have the power to rewrite it. What you have been through and are going through does not determine your identity. It does not determine the qualities you have or the essence of your being and who you are. You are unique, and your story was tailor-made just for you. Even though what you experienced seems unfair and has been painful, there is meaning and purpose in what has been the toxicity of your life.

The memories may never go away because they have left scars on your heart and in your mind. However, let those scars be the source of your motivation to mend your broken pieces. Every chapter in your life has been written through your life cycles. You and those around you have read every chapter. You are not defined by what has happened to you or what you have done. However, what defines you is how you allow yourself to shift into place and maximize your life right now.

Although your story has been toxic, you can rid the toxins by removing all the negative thoughts associated with the guilt, shame, rejection, hurt, and pain of your trauma. Begin to rewrite your story by intertwining yourself in your healing process. Although your story started off as a damaged narrative, allow the pen of your healing to scribe the ending that speaks to you being a conqueror, a champion, an overcomer, a victor. Why? Because your story does not define you.

You must know and believe that you can rewrite your story. Although your trauma happened *to* you, you must know that it happened *for* you. It happened for you to live to tell your story, show you how strong you are, and how your strength will impact someone else's healing journey. You made it through it and are still living today.

How do you rewrite your story? First, challenge every negative thought associated with your trauma. Challenge every negative thought you speak and have spoken over your life and your life story. Drown out that noise and bring those thoughts into captivity. Remember, you are not what or who others say you are. You are who *you* say you are. You are not what happened to you. You are a victor, not a victim. Say to yourself things that speak life and healing to your heart and mind.

End every chapter in your life that doesn't serve you anymore—people and things—get rid of them. Begin to adjust your vision. See yourself as more than your situation, more than your abuse, more than your rejection, more than your loss, more than your mistake, more than your hurt and pain. See yourself as the strong person you are. See yourself as the best version of YOU. See yourself accomplishing your dreams and smiling while you are on top of the mountain. Because you have hiked up through all the rough edges, you are now on the top of the mountain, gazing down at the green pasture. From that vantage point, you can now see a bright future.

End every chapter in your life that doesn't serve you anymore.

Change your narrative and begin to be what you want to be, even if you can't completely do it the way you desire. Well, how do you do that? You do it by practicing it now. You won't be your best self until you start practicing being your best self. You can't wait until things change in your life that you want to change. You can't keep waiting for the prime time and opportunity. The time and opportunity are now. You are enough, and you will always be enough. Start walking and talking like you have arrived at the version of you that makes you feel good. Yes, I know that's hard because your self-confidence and self-esteem have not quite risen to the occasion. Fake it until you make it. Walk in it and talk in it like it has manifested. Before you know it, it will.

Your story does not define you. You are so much more than your circumstances. You just have to believe it. Let go of every old definition that you have come up with that is contrary to you living and feeling your best. Redefine who you are. Run faster than all your fears as if you were running for your life—because you are. Become entangled and intrigued with the thoughts of what you can actually do. And, do it because you can.

You can do whatever you put your mind to. Daydream and envision your life looking like and being what you have always desired it to be. Play it out in your mind and plan how you can get there. See yourself winning and not allowing your life to just happen. You make your life happen. So, live to the fullest and on purpose. You only get one life. You have to see yourself winning because, sometimes, others can't.

You don't have to be perfect. Remember, no perfect people allowed. Wake up wanting to do better every single day. Try to at least be 1% better than you were the day before. That equals progress. Continue to progress. Lastly, stop blaming others and what happened to you. Stop blaming the mistakes that you have made. Stop allowing them to stagnate you and keep you stuck in the tight fist of fear and unproductivity. Instead, rise to the occasion. Stand proud in everything you have done and that has happened to you. Yes, your trauma was real. It's a painful memory, and it doesn't and didn't feel good. Yet, your story does not define you. You are a victor, not a victim. So, I challenge you to stand victorious today and every day!

CHAPTER CHALLENGE

How will you redefine your story? What will your healing say about you? What will you say about yourself now after reading this book?

Write It Out

....

....

....

....

....

....

....

....

....

....

....

....

....

....

....

....

....

....

....

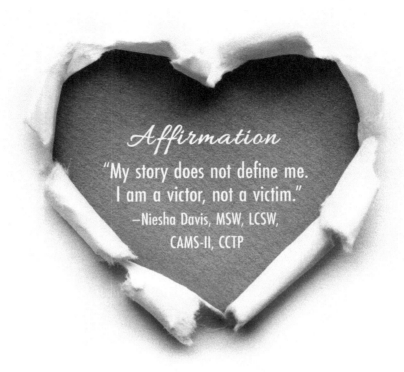

Affirmation
"My story does not define me.
I am a victor, not a victim."
—Niesha Davis, MSW, LCSW,
CAMS-II, CCTP

SELF-AFFIRMATION

Write out your own affirmation after reading this chapter. Make a commitment to challenge yourself to say it today and when you need to be reminded and reaffirmed.

....

....

....

....

....

....

Acknowledgments

I want to first thank God for allowing me to write this book and share it with you. Without Him, there would be no me.

I want to thank my publisher, Christian Living Books, Inc., for making my book come alive and be tangible for all to see. Kimberly Stewart, you are the best.

I want to thank my mother and father for raising me to be the woman I am today. You both have been instrumental in my life and have always wanted me to do and be my best.

I want to say thank you to my siblings, Vance, Yvette, Jay, Lamorris, Previs, and Shavon, for always being so supportive in everything that I do. I love you all.

I want to thank my girls that I can say have been my true friends in every stage of my life. Donica and Pat, you have been in my life for years and are my sisters. You are the true definition of friends. I truly appreciate you two. Thank you for always being supportive, encouraging, and loving me in everything. Thank you for being there for me… no matter what. Keep shining!

To Mrs. Ruthie, thank you for being a role model, a mentor, an auntie, and a friend! You have been very instrumental in me developing into the woman I am today. Your wisdom and knowledge have been so rich and have provided so much guidance in my life. You making me laugh and smile to keep from crying has been a great coping mechanism. I know you got me, and I thank you.

To Miriam and Pam, thank you for also being my friends. I appreciate you both. You are great women in your own right.

I appreciate everything you have imparted into my life, and I salute you. Thank you to my YWRAP crew, Miriam, Dawntina, and Tabitha. I appreciate all the support you have given to me through the years. I so appreciate you all for believing in me and trusting me. I appreciate you for always having my back and also being good friends.

To Charoletta and Voncile, thank you for being my cheerleaders and helping me to see me. You two have always supported me and wished the best for me. Voncile, you have always cheered me on and celebrated me in all my endeavors. Thank you for all my therapy sessions in your chair.

Thank you to my church family. Thank you, Bishop Vernon and Lady Vicki Kemp, for being great leaders and trusting me. Lady Kemp, thank you for cheering me on and being supportive and creative. Thank you for being willing and ready to help in any way you can. I salute you, Lady Kemp.

Thank you to everyone who has been instrumental in my life in some form or fashion. I appreciate you. I appreciate everyone who has believed in me and the visions that God has given me. I appreciate everyone who has supported me through the years.

Thank you to everyone who took the time to purchase this book. I pray that it has blessed you and has pushed you to the next level of your healing journey.

About the Author

Niesha Davis owns two mental health practices in Bakersfield, California: Life Connections and InspireMe Counseling and Wellness Center. She is the founder and CEO of YWRAP (Young Women Reaching Accomplishable Places), a mentorship program for at-risk girls. Niesha is a strong advocate for mental health and the mentally ill. Also, she is an author, a therapist, a consultant, motivational speaker, and facilitator.

She has a Bachelor of Science degree in Criminal Justice and a Master's in Social Work. She is a Licensed Clinical Social Worker, a Licensed Evangelist, a Certified Anger Management Specialist II, and a Certified Clinical Trauma Professional. She is also certified as a Mental Health provider for women who suffer from perinatal/postnatal mood disorders.

Niesha was born and raised in Bakersfield, CA. She has been helping individuals, children, and families for over 20 years in Human Services, Case Management, Social Work, and Psychotherapy. She has also worked as a medical social worker with patients/families on dialysis, in hospice, in a psychiatric mental health facility, within the legal system in corrections, and in education as a School Social Worker.

Niesha has a wealth of experience in many areas, including Child Protective Services, group homes, family resource centers, children and adults with developmental disabilities, adolescents, single mothers, and pregnant women.

She loves her community, has a passion for helping others, and strives to help everyone she can to fulfill their dreams. Niesha says, "It's okay not to be okay. We all need someone who gives us the courage, strength, guidance, and support to get through challenges in life. Someone who we can connect with, who we can trust, who can identify with our needs in a safe place. Each day, I am blessed to be that someone for children, adolescents, parents, women, couples, and families. I walk with them and work through those challenges, which can be so scary and overwhelming. I am passionate about empowering individuals with the tools they need to improve their overall quality of life. I believe that if we plant positive seeds and continue to water them, eventually, a harvest will grow. My goal in working with individuals and families is to see them transition from a place of not just surviving but to thriving."

Niesha is on a mission to break the stigma associated with mental health and mental illness. She encourages all to get professional help when needed. Her work is her passion. She considers her work in the therapy room to be ministry and feels honored and blessed to be a psychotherapist.

Connect with the Author

- ⓘ   Nieshadavislcsw
- 🅵   Lifeconnect2
- ◉   Lifeconnections.email
- ✉   Info@lifeconnections.email

9 781562 295677